# Thoughts of a Single Mother

*The Reflections of My Soul*

Lisa Renee
Hutchins

# Contents

# CONTEMPLATION

# SELF-RESPECT

# ABSENCE

## DEAR MOTHERS

## POSITIVE RELATIONS

## LOVE AS WE GROW

# SELF-LOVE

# Inspiration

My children have molded me into the mother and woman I am today. They gave me the strength to endure the struggles, storms, and blessings of being a single mother. They taught me that I had to pull my life and emotions together because they depended on me to be a leader, a provider, and a role model. Their laughter, acceptance, and actions showed me what I needed to change in our environment to provide a healthier home with a happy and strong mother. Instead of the damaged person I was becoming. Thank you, Jordan and Summer, for blessing me beyond measure and loving me through it all.

# Dear Single Mothers

Mothers know today that you are beautiful, amazing, and strive every day to be your best. As a single parent, life may have turned out to be a rusty, old, broken fence when you thought it would be a white picket fence! But everything happens for a reason. We have to learn from the fences that appeared incredible but turned out to be rotten. We also have to keep walking by the broken fences and resist the urge to fix them in order to find the fence made for us. We must take responsibility for wearing the wrong shoes along the way. Those old, dirty lawn mowing shoes will not take us anywhere but back to old fences. So, look in the mirror each day and remind yourself that you have to build your own fence alone, with your children first in order to receive the right fence built for you!

I thank you for taking the time to read my thoughts on being a single mother. You will laugh, cry, feel empowered, and learn that the struggles of being a single mother do not have to define you. They are lessons molding you into the woman you were designed to be.

# Young Love

# Love

Sees no color
Sees no age

Does not hurt
Does not lie

Can't be rushed
Can't be forced

Love is happiness
Love is meaningful

Symbolizes commitment
Symbolizes honesty

Requires patience
Requires forgiveness

# The One

You wonder your whole life about your husband or wife
Who they will be
What they will look like
And what they will do


You wonder when you'll find each other
When you are young
When you are old
When you are happy
Or when you are sad


But it's when you stop wondering
They find you
They put you first
Loving you endlessly

They are just what you imagined

The best friend

The lover

The soul mate you dreamed of


You know they are the one by

The spiritual connection

The security

The honesty

And the unconditional commitment

# Spontaneous Wind

You gently blew into my life unexpectedly

Stirring up unfamiliar feelings

Rearranging my perspective

Changing my direction

Calming my uncertainty

Settling my mind

# Love Senses

A slight glance filled with passion
The eyes capture the emotions burning inside

A soothing sound of internal flames igniting
The ears sense a melody
That softens their souls

A gentle smell of roses
The nose fills with the scent of attraction

A slight flavor of a first kiss
The mouths connect with the taste of strawberry compassion

An embrace that feels so right
The touch that overflows their hearts with love

# Fireside

One quiet afternoon, she is relaxing on her couch
Cuddling with her blanket next to the fireplace
Peacefully sipping her hot chocolate


Reminiscing about their first date at a coffee shop
Toasting their mochas
Eating pastries
Enjoying the instant connections they shared


Bringing a smile to her face
As the butterflies of love start fluttering
Warming her heart


In the midst of her new happiness
Anticipating their next encounter
She receives a text from him inviting her to dinner
Overjoyed, she accepts
In hopes for this opportunity at love

# Deception

# Sunday

He quietly opens the door
He looks to his left, and there she is


Standing at the top of the stairs
Wearing a short, white, fuzzy bathrobe
That is slightly opened
Revealing her sexy white lingerie


Her soft brown hair is curled perfectly
As her vanilla skin shimmers in the candlelight
Her jewelry glistens
Her stilettos accent her long, sexy legs
As he slowly walks up the stairs
Mesmerized by her beauty

He touches her smooth skin
She slowly leads him to the bedroom
The aroma of roses fills the air
The candles slowly burning
While their shadows silhouette in the distance


They passionately undress one other
Caressing their bodies


She softly lays him on the bed
Gently sitting on top of him


Massaging his neck with her tongue
He embraces her body


She moves to his soft brown lips
Passionately kissing and sucking them gently


His body grows longer
As her hands begin to caress it

Thoughts of a Single Mother

She slithers her tongue down his chest
Kisses around his lower stomach
Then, places her mouth around him

With her hand and mouth moving together
He softly moans for more

He grabs her hair to get a better view
Yearning for her body

She slowly climbs on top
Shifting her hips back and forth
Pressing her chest against his

She wraps her arms around his neck
To get a better grip

He smacks her ass as it quickly moves

Up and down

Pounding against him


She softly whispers her desires

He releases, slithers down and gently latches on

She gently grabs the pillows in pure pleasure


As he touches and licks

Her breath gets short and loud

She quickly whispers her need to feel him


He lays her on her back

Holds her legs over his arms and starts penetrating

Her body instantly throbs for more


As he massages her spot

He leans in, holding her tightly

Gently pulling her hair

She begins to talk dirty

Thoughts of a Single Mother


They wait for each other

Reaching ecstasy as one


They slowly relax

Get dressed and kiss goodbye


He goes back to his family

And she goes back to being the other woman

# Who Is She?

They sit down to enjoy a relaxing evening

Snuggling on the couch

Eating popcorn, waiting for the movie to start


His phone notification goes off

Not concerned

He asks his girlfriend to check his phone


Instantly her heart drops

As she sees another girl sending kiss emojis

Thanking him for last night


The anger erupts

As he denies the accusation, storming out of the room

Confirming his recent unengaged behavior

Was for a reason

# Representatives

Are masks people wear
Hiding their true intentions
Behind a charming smile
Falsely promising a secure future


Only to secretly take off each mask
One disappointment at a time
Blaming their shortcomings on others
Taking no accountability for their deception

# True Colors

When a person gets angry
True colors are revealed


Hearts may turn to stone
Prideful attitudes may detour from solutions
Reactions may become invisible
Aggressive touching may instill fear
Defensiveness decreases understanding


Or


Their hearts may reveal honesty
Attitudes may encourage openness
Reactions may create an easy solution
Touch may instill support and encouragement
Understanding may allow for a stronger connection


True colors reveal a person's inner ability
To control their emotions

# Darkness Behind Closed Doors

As you're yelling damaging words
You are hardening the very heart
You once healed


As the anger rages with no remorse
You are changing the caring image
You once portrayed


As you stare right through me
You are creating a shell of emotionless feelings
You once removed


As you physically pull away
You are distancing the comfort
You once welcomed

As the tension grows thicker
You are closing the heart
You once opened


As you strike me
You end the love
You once received

# The Fiery Slap

SLAP!
Instantly, the fire ignites
Staring the towering man in the face

Quickly lashing back
The fire blows through the hallway

Clear liquid attempts to put out the fire
But it grows, swarming through the house

The aggressiveness of the fire instantly stops
As a powerful blow disintegrates the flames

The ashes lay lifeless

But the fire still burns inside the foundation


The only way to put out the fire completely

Is forgiveness

# Waves in the Storm

Every couple disagrees
They get hurt, upset, and maybe even cry

But it's how they disagree
That shows their commitment to love

Their ability to control their tempers
Their willingness to be open-minded

Their desire to forgive and comfort one another
Their acceptance to agree on a concrete solution

Their ability to move forward
Without looking back

# Contemplation

# The Currents of Love

The way we vibe feels like home
Your endless laughter warms my soul
The love for music makes our bodies
Overflow with passion

When you text me
I can finish your thoughts as easy as I breathe

I felt my heart opening to receive your affection
Enjoying possibilities
I put on the shelf

I start trusting you enough to share my fears
Making me feel like I was flying again

Then, all of a sudden
You shot me right out of the sky

Showing me you have an angry appetite

To control my actions


Attacking my abilities to provide for my children

Setting demands I can't meet

With no compassion for my situation


Sternly attempting to enforce your demands

With heartless ultimatums


I attempt to warn you

But the accusations of mistrust spew like fire


Burning my skin, flame by flame

Attempting to reopen scars I already healed


I refuse to walk forward through similar fires

I already put out

## Thoughts of a Single Mother

So, I sit here wondering why
You are not taking my warnings

The fire from your breath is sweltering
I need your water to soothe me
Or the undertows in my ocean will pull me into silence

So, I choose to walk away from you
Before my words burn your skin in return

In attempts to save the passionate remains
But is it enough to sustain the currents of love

# Caught In the Middle

Do you stay for the family?
Denying the need for a genuine relationship.


Do you leave for the positive potential of the unknown?
Risking another broken heart.


Either choice will ignite an internal struggle.
Selfishness, excitement, doubt, peace, and stress


You will grow in wisdom,
Or crumble with bitterness.


Do not settle as the losses heal.
The right choice is one's happiness.

# Conscious

In life, we yearn to do things we shouldn't.


Is it the intensified temptation?
The lack of self-control?
Or maybe we just try to go outside of our box,
Knowing we may regret what we do.


The curiosity of the unknown is often irresistible.


Is it the heightened suspense?
The failure of resistance?
Or maybe we want to see the fantasy as reality,
Knowing we may be disappointed.

The conscious is a red flag warning us to be cautious.


Is it the words of wisdom?

The disregard of self-worth?

Or maybe we want a fairy tale experience,

Knowing it doesn't exist.

# Unfamiliar Touch

When you looked at me
I felt the old you


When you touched me
I felt the love
I once knew


When you hugged me
I felt your coldness melt away


When you kissed me
I felt my body wanting you to stay


When your touch went away
I felt your affection close the door

When you walked away

I felt an understanding

That our connection was no more

# Truth

What is truth?
A Choice
The whole truth can be revealed,
Or just enough to cover the hidden scandal.


Why is the truth revealed?
Freedom
The release of a guilty conscience,
Or exposing a mistake that encourages healing.


When should the truth be told?
Always
The secret will constantly distract one's focus,
Or create distance in a relationship.

Where should the truth be exposed?

Anywhere

The privacy of one's home,

Or in front of millions of people.


How is truth told?

Honestly

The sincerity of a confessional conversation,

Or a revealing letter that encourages a response.

# Hiding Inside

She knows deep inside
The relationship won't work
No matter how hard she tries


But she holds her doubts inside
Hoping that as long as she does not say them out loud
All the complaining and heartache will work itself out


Wanting one day
For him to appreciate everything she has done


Making all the pain
Worth staying together

# Crossroads

Do you do what's convenient?
Or what's right?


Do you take a chance?
Or stay unhappy?


Do you follow your heart?
Or settle?


Do what's right.
Or have regrets and settle for less.

# Brittle Foundation

Trust is like a house
It starts with a foundation


From there, the house takes form
It can be built quickly, or slow, and steady


When the house is consistently
Destroyed and rebuilt
Unwanted walls begin to build


When these walls are challenged, they cause
Unnecessary anger, frustration, and mistrust
Generating a fire that swarms through the foundation

As the fire intensifies, the trust disintegrates

Eventually, there will be nothing left but ashes


The only way to restore the foundation

Is a new house

# Letting Go

Saying goodbye
Crying about being alone


Collecting old memorabilia in a box
Freeing your mind of the reminders
Resisting from making that phone call


Walking around with your head up
Reassuring yourself that it will get better


Realizing what went wrong
Learning about yourself


Allowing time for closure
Meeting new people
And starting over

# Self-Respect

# The Shouting of Silence

The silence of her phone was a reality check
The feeling of honest rejection
A painful reminder of her haunting past

The devaluing of extending sex for pleasure
Masking a lonely need to be desired

The disappointment of realizing
They were not even friends
A naive girl thinking a guy
Could actually want more than sex

The silence was needed to stop her
From chasing something with no end

# The Drivers' Seat

Control is power

Power places you in

The driver's seat


When one's power is challenged

The driver feels weak

The weakness triggers a need to regain control


If power is used to regain control

All control is lost

And your power has no meaning

# Entangled in the Webs

The silence shouts, "You are disposable."
"Your friendship was just to see what I could get."
"Now that I got it or discovered the truth, NEXT!"
"I don't care what happened; it just doesn't work for me."


Now, how do you feel?
Maybe you just move on to the next
Never reflecting on what you are doing to yourself


Maybe you realize you're spinning an un-weavable web
Never satisfied as you are caught in a web of unfulfilling desires


Maybe you are just doing what everyone else is doing
Knowing in your heart it's not you


Whatever it may be
STOP!

Put yourself first

Respect your body


The right man will come

Just be patient

# Damage Vs Truth

Confines hearts   vs   Frees souls

Denies growth   vs   Encourages change

Opens scars   vs   Heals wounds


Continues generational curses   vs   Inspires change

Creates denial   vs   Develops perspectives


Ignites heartache   vs   Sparks love

Destroys trust   vs   Strengthens foundations

Generates walls   vs   Exposes reality

# Love Yourself Enough

Love yourself enough
To set boundaries
Do what's right
Even if it hurts


Love yourself enough
To be the role model
God designed you to be
Even if it means sacrificing your wants for needs


Love yourself enough
To build a legacy
Worth following
Even if you have to do it yourself

# Scars of a Survivor

The scars are everywhere
Some are visible
Causing others to question
Seeing our trauma's consequences every day


Others are hiding under our clothes
Calloused and healed on the surface
But sensitive to the world around us


Then, there are the wounds within
Invisible to others and sometimes ourselves
Still bleeding at the slightest triggers


Despite all these scars
A survivor finds a way to heal all these wounds
Not to be defined by the damage
But to be an advocate for helping others overcome

# Absence

# Selfish Ghost

Making no time for his child
Prioritizing himself first


Twisting stories
Making the responsible parent look bad


Generating excuses to justify his actions
Easily forgetting financial obligations


Working under the table saying,
"I'll get around to it."


Taking credit for his son's success
Secretly knowing
He does not truly "know" his child


Randomly buying toys
Appearing as the hero

Filling his son's head with broken promises
Knowing his mother has to heal
His wounds of disappointment


Be better for your son
Because he didn't choose you

# Missing Out

While you are celebrating your home run
Your son wonders why
You are missing all of his


While you are eagerly enjoying the nightlife
Your son is sadly wanting you
To read him a bedtime story


While you are loving other women
Your son is yearning for your affection
Just one more time


While you are committed to watching TV
Your son is questioning why
You can't watch his favorite movie with him

While you are sleeping in every Sunday
Your son looks around at church seeing everyone
But you


While you carelessly work under the table
Your son is complaining about me working late


While you give your heart to everyone
But him


Your son is unconditionally
Committed to loving you

# The Mirrors Reflection

The day will come
When she sees the real you


She'll see the fake shell
That gently surrounds you


As time cracks the shell
It will reveal a lost soul
Who is always one step away
From spiraling out of control


Watching your damaged heart
Burn bridge after bridge
Destroying everyone in your path
Then, quickly moving on to your next victim

One day, there will be no one left
Your family and friends will say goodbye
The children will move away
Many closing the doors to your affection


Even the baby girl
You pushed aside
Teaching her that loving you hurts


The only one waiting for you at the end
Will be your reflection

# Who Is He?

Mom, do I have a dad?

Yes, you do.


Where is he?

I do not know, honey.


What happened?

We divorced, and he disagreed with the plan.


Was he there?

No.


Could he have changed it?

Yes.


Why doesn't he see me?

Because he disagrees.

Seven years later…

Mom, is that my dad?
Yes.

I am happy to get to know him!
I am as well, but protect your heart.

Why mom?
Because not every parent can handle being a parent.

Mom, why does he say those things?
Well, we all have our own ways of co-parenting.

Why doesn't he love me?
All parents love in their own way.

Why doesn't he respond?
Accepting who he is will make it easier when he doesn't respond.

Mom, thank you,

For teaching me how to love myself more.


Self-worth and taking your power back,

Is the key to happiness.

# Tribulations of the Law

Who complains about providing?
A parent that is not present.


Who calls yelling when you receive a check?
A parent getting caught for working under the table.


Who does all the work to get support?
A parent not getting help for their child.


Who provides proof for justice?
A parent just trying to make it.


Who gets child support randomly?
A parent that trusts the system.


Who gives financial credit where it's due?
A parent that believes in fairness.

# Entitlement

Being a father in a child's eye
Is not an entitlement
It's earned


One day at a time
Consistently showing up
In the presence of their hardships and successes


Guiding them when they need directions
Cheering them through their success
Encouraging them to follow their dreams


Showing them that your relationship is undeniable
Healthy co-parenting is possible
And your love is just one call away

# Stepping In

Another man may step into your shoes
Providing for your child
Emotionally and financially


Happily being present daily
In the midst of your consistent absence


The accountability is on you
To maintain your bond with your child


Not to be resentful
Creating hardships for everyone


But to swallow your pride and work together
Showing him appreciation
For loving and guiding your child as his own

# The Monster

He finds ways to create turmoil
In an effort to be seen as the hero
Searching for praise from a child
He constantly disappoints


Putting the mother in a bad position
Knowing she will say no
In an effort to be the good guy
Not realizing he is only hurting his child in the end


Reinforcing generational family curses
Not realizing he is instilling subconscious family norms
Just to be able to laugh in the faces of the people he once loved

# Dear Mothers

# Positive

---

"Ma'am, you are pregnant"
"What do you want to do?"
My eyes glazed over in disbelief.
My heart sank, and I was speechless.
I sat there thinking,
"I can't have a baby right now."


The nurse handed me some papers and said,
"Here are some resources of your options
for an abortion or becoming a mother."
"Make a follow-up appointment at the front desk."
"Good luck, and I'm sorry."


I slowly picked up my things,
got into my car,
And drove home crying.


As the tears rolled down my face,
My body filled with anxiety.

My thoughts raced endlessly.

"I finally got away from his dad, and now I am pregnant?"

If I tell him, he will want to get back together!!"

"My parents are going to kill me!!!!"

"How will I be a single mom and attend grad school?"

Overwhelmed with a life-changing decision,

I prayed, called my friend's mom, and made an appointment.

I was an emotional wreck the next week.

The day came, and I hesitantly checked in at the clinic.

The lobby was filled with baby donations,

Information for new mothers, and a stroller.

I sat there thinking,

"I can't believe this is happening."

"Lisa? Hi, ma'am, follow me.

How are you feeling?"

I timidly said,

"I'm ok."

"We are going to take a look to see how far along you are
Before you make any decisions."
As she looked for the baby, I was in shock.


All of a sudden
I heard a heartbeat.
The doctor said,
"There is your baby. You are six weeks."


Instantly, my heart decided.
I was going to become a mother.
"Here is a little picture of your baby."


As I walked out with a small smile,
I knew the road was going to be hard.


I was not sure where to start,
But I knew I had to begin planning.

Telling my family,

the father,

My best friend.


The disappointment was heavy,

Devastating many.


But despite the heartache,

I had to embrace my journey.

# Reactions of Discouragement

---

"WHAT!!!!!!!!!!!!!!!!!!!!!!!!!!!!!!!!!!!"

"WWWWWTTTTTTTTFFFFFFFFFF!"

"You CAN'T have that baby!"
"How are you going to have a baby and graduate?!!!"

"How are you going to go to grad school?"
"You will be a loser the rest of your life."
"Well, I guess you can't move to Hawaii now?"

"What Happened? I thought you broke up?"
"Are you going to tell him?"
"Do you even want to be with him again?"

"What are you going to do?"

"Are you going to move out of your sorority and back home?"


"Did your dad get mad at who the dad was?"

"Was he ok with the baby being mixed?"

"You know it is hard to have a blended family, right?"

# Motherhood

Being a mother doesn't mean
She has to be mistreated
Verbally destroyed for setting expectations


Being a mother doesn't mean
She has to support the family alone
Struggling with a financially inconsistent partner


Being a mother doesn't mean
She is responsible for the father's personal needs
Knowing they are no longer together


Being a mother doesn't mean
She has to lose herself
Ignoring her purpose to please everyone else

Being a mother doesn't mean
She has to stay in the relationship
Being trapped because they have a child


Only to sacrifice everything
For a father who is never going to show up
For their children or themselves

# Single Parent Shame

Do your kids have the same dad?

No.

Do they see their dads?

No.

Where are your babies' daddies?

I don't know.

Do you care?

I care about what I can control.

I can control myself,

my attitude,

The love I share with my children.

I can change my reactions,

my resentment,

Show them how to laugh in the midst of the struggle.


But I can't fill a void,

That was not meant for me to fill.

# The Burning Glare of a Stranger

A glare begins burning through my back

As I turn around

I see a lady

Who recognizes me

But I don't know her


Then I see him

My soon-to-be ex-husband

Who just left my house a week ago


While she smiles proudly, spending her money

Buying him a new wardrobe

Our daughter starts calling for her dad

He ignores her excitement and presence


As I stand there in shock

My blood is boiling

My heart is shattered

Our daughter is confused

I quickly distract her
As they check out
Walking away laughing


I stand there paralyzed
By his complete disregard
For our family
For our daughter


I find a smile to mask my pain
But that glare of a stranger
Burns my soul

# The Blind Reality of Heartlessness

An unexpected check came in the mail
Surprisingly, it was child support
What a blessing at the right time


The next day, the phone rang
It was the girlfriend of my son's dad
Who I never met
She asked for some of the money


Sitting in shock, trying to control my reaction
I introduced myself and asked her,
"Do you know how much daycare costs?"
She said,
"No, I don't have kids."


I told her as calmly as I could,
"This is my first child support check in 5 years.
His son's daycare bill comes every month."

She was quiet, and I told her,

"I can't help you and wish you the best."


I hung up, thinking to myself,

"What kind of person does that?"


Someone who does not have their life together

Pray for them and stay strong

# Angel of Forgiveness

My mind is overwhelmed with devastation
Knowing I have to decide


My heart bleeds with sadness
Knowing I am choosing to let you fly


My body trembles
Knowing I will never hold you in my arms


My eyes stream endless tears
Knowing I will never see your smile


My ears pound with the silence
Knowing I will never hear your voice


My hands reach to the sky
Knowing I need forgiveness

If I am granted his grace

Knowing I betrayed your life


My heart will be forever grateful

Knowing I may have a chance to see you one day

# A Child's Broken Reality

Sharing the truth of separation
Can cut a deeper scar
Or relieves a child from false realities


Showing compassion for loss
Can create a tailspin of misunderstanding
Or bring a child closer to you


Discussing reasons for absence
Can build walls of resentment
Or help a child accept their life


Revealing your mistakes
Can foster bitter grudges
Or show a child we all fall short


Empowering forgiveness
Can ignite a fiery of anger
Or bring a child closure

# The Tree in the Distance

Letting out your feelings
Plants the seed


Creating positive self-talk
Encourages the tree to grow


Achieving your goals
Pushes the tree through the dirt


Feeling positive about yourself
Provides the water to help your branches grow


Learning from your mistakes
Confirms that no storm can knock you over


Realizing you are in control of your future
Turns you into a strong and powerful tree
For the whole world to see

# The Door at the End of the Road

The road to the door looked dark
As it stared you in the face


The road was cold and appeared endless
As you stepped onto it for the first time


The road was overwhelming and provided no direction
As you pushed up the hills


The road made unexpected turns
As you dug in your heels and held on tight


The road tried to throw you off
As the determination burned inside


The road became straighter
As you learned how to steer

The road became brighter
As you continued to drive forward
Through the cloudy days


The road finally ended
As you opened the door


Your children stood their smiling
Making the rough road worth it

# The First

The first time I held you, my heart filled with joy
I was blessed you were healthy


The first time you smiled
I was amazed by your excitement


The first time you laughed
Jenny and I tried to make you do it again


The first time you walked
All I could do was cheer


The first time you spoke
I couldn't wait to hear you say mama


The first time you fell
I was there to pick you up

The first day of school
I cried with tears of joy


The first time you played basketball
I knew you would love the game


The first time you liked a girl
I was excited to hear your thoughts


The first time you had a bad day
I was motivated to make you feel good


The first time you made a mistake
I was encouraged to show you what was right

The first time you succeeded on your own

I was proud of your accomplishment


The first time you realized that you could change your life

I knew that you were going to be a superstar

# Thirteen

The road to adulthood begins
You will grow a man stash


You will wake up one day
Sounding like a man


You will be gone soon
Hanging out with your friends


You will have a girlfriend
You will even stop hugging me in public


But you are always going to be my little Jordan
Someone who makes my sad days happy
Someone who makes me laugh
Someone who makes me proud

# Accepting Your New Direction

One stormy night, your life took a sharp turn
Suddenly and unexpectedly

You were disoriented, looking for answers
Trying to make sense of what was transpiring

We all reacted in fear
Trying to embrace you

The night became dark
The thunder rolled

As we drove down the road, your smile surfaced
While you were singing to the radio

The tears were swelling in my eyes
Slowly rolling down my left cheek

As I quickly reassured you everything was ok
You trusted me


Accepting your new direction, paving your success
No matter how unexpected the road was ahead

# Renewing a Faded Star

When you were little
You shinned like a star


Your stories made me laugh
Your hugs melted my pain away
Your feistiness kept me on my toes


As time passed
The trauma of life changed your heart


Your smile disappeared
Your entertainment faded
Your desire to communicate evaporated


The love you used to share was locked away
Behind this cloud of sadness
My shining star turned dim

Let me blow away your storm

To renew the shining star

Healing the wounds that stole your light

# You Changed Me

When you were little
I thought you only saw the happy, loving mother
I was on the outside


But you are the only one
Who saw the damaged person
I was on the inside


Showing me a reflection of what
I was not trying to teach


Revealing the image
I was hiding


Igniting my journey to healing
Forever changing me as a mother
From the inside out

Making me a better person for you

Just by loving me

Through it all

# Gummers

You make Mommy smile
When you call me Momers


You make Mommy laugh
When you tell me stories about school


You make Mommy happy
When you dance around


You make Mommy proud
When you make good choices


You make Mommy feel loved
When you give me big hugs


You make Mommy grateful
Because life would never be the same without you

# The Thankless Sacrifice

Day in and day out
The single mother is grinding away


Ensuring the children stay on track
Racing them here and there
After a long, strenuous day at work


Quietly crying inside for a break
Yearning for a hug
A friendly reminder that she is doing her best
Even if she is struggling to carry the weight alone


Hoping just once he would call
To care about the kids
Coordinate a time to see them
Maybe thanking her for all she has done without him

# It's Not the End

Being a single parent is not the end
Even though it was never the goal

You may not have the flexibility
To come and go as you please

You may not get much time alone
To care for your personal needs

You may end up staying single
To protect your children from further damage

But choosing peace
Is a priceless way
To show your children they come first

# Positive Relations

# A Special Friend

In life, we meet people every day
Some pass by
And others become acquaintances


Then there are those
With whom we automatically connect
We form an instant bond


As time passes
We share stories that expose our souls
Jokes are told, laughter is contagious
Enjoying each other becomes a routine


As hard times approach
Support and understanding comes naturally
We give advice
Encouraging each other to stay strong

Sacrificing is easy

Because we want to share in each other's success

We are open and honest

Keeping the friendship true


A special friend is hard to find

But I found that in you

# Our Journey

We started out as two cheerleaders
On top of the world
Naive to the actual realities of life


We lost our flowers and went to college
Realizing we were lost souls
Trying to find our way
Through the newfound freedoms


We expanded our minds
Beyond their narrow paths


We experienced the joys and pains of relationships
We even let our hair down
Enjoyed being young


Then, my path took a sharp turn
But you held my hand all the way

We were in different chapters
But our friendship still remained


We gained wisdom
Learned how to improve ourselves
Through self-reflection and honesty


You reminded me of my youth
Every time you took me out


Now, we are young women
Who know what we are doing
And where we are going


Tomorrow remains a mystery
But our friendship is predictable


The shape changes
But the foundation stays the same

# Helping the Silent Soldier

As her son was getting bigger
He needed a dresser for his clothes
But she didn't have the money


She said a short prayer to herself
Hoping God would send her a sign


Later that day
She walked outside to take out the trash
There, next to the dumpster
Sat a children's dresser
With a "Free" sign on it


She was hesitant to look at it
Not ever considering taking things from the trash


She went on with her day
But that dresser was lingering in her mind

She went into her bedroom
Quietly looking at it through her window


Swallowing her pride
She decided to go check it out


Slowly walking down the stairs
In hopes none of the neighbors would see her


She quickly inspected the dresser
To her surprise
It was clean
All the drawers worked
And it was scratch-free


Struggling to try and lift it alone
A nice lady started walking her way
With a garbage bag and a children's bed frame

Thoughts of a Single Mother

She laughed in embarrassment
Saying she was just looking at it


With a huge smile
The lady offered to give her everything


Her son's old bed set to match
The garbage bag full of toddler clothes
Even offering to help her carry it


A smile beamed across her face
Thankful that someone was nice enough to help her
She offered the lady a few dollars
But the lady was just happy to pass it on to someone


With excitement
She cleaned the dresser
Filling it with all the new clothes
Setting up his new bed
Waiting for grandma to drop him off from church

He was so excited about his new bed
The dresser was easy for him to open
Enjoying the new airplane pajamas


She tucked her son into his new bed
Happy to be able to provide what he needed
Thanking God for the blessings
She had to be humble enough to receive

# Your Hands Healed My Heart

Your hands
Gently removed the walls around my heart
Piece by piece

Your hands
Slowly opened the locked doors
One by one

Your hands
Surrounded my wounds with honesty and understanding
Conversation by conversation

Your hands
Introduced your heart to mine
Minute by minute

Your hands
Intertwined our souls
Day by day


Your hands
Restored my heart
Beat by beat

# Your Wings

Your Wings
Softly comforted my damaged soul


Your Wings
Roughly brushed my life with reality


Your Wings
Bravely protected me from harm


Your Wings
Swiftly covered me when I needed you most


Your Wings
Gently embarrassed me with happiness


Your Wings
Created a nest of unforgettable memories

# Same Side of the Table

The new girlfriend is amazing
Believing the lies he tells
Assuming the mothers are to blame


For the broken relationship
His absence in his children's lives
His lack of willingness to co-parent
Trusting she will make it all better


Only to discover
She is now eating from the same side of the table
As all the other mother's
Turning perceived enemies into friends


Experiencing first hand
The unhealthy realities of his ways
Harshly understanding why
Raising his children alone is best for everyone
Until his children learn to love him with a grain of salt

# Scars of Laughter

One sunny Friday evening after work
Two friends share a bottle of wine
Laughing about the scars of the past


The lack of child support
Going to food banks
Attending free school supply church events
Getting children's hand-me-down clothes from other parents


The drama with new girlfriends
Attempting to be the hero
Assuming you were the problem
Only to realize the mother is open to being friends


Toasting to healing from their single-parent trauma
Celebrating the obstacles they overcame together

# Love As We Grow

# The Way

The way you look at me
Makes my body melt
I yearn for your touch


My mind fantasizes about
What I want to do to you


I gently touch your hands
Pulling you close to me


I kiss your soft lips
Caressing your smooth back


I softly take off your shirt
While I kiss your muscular chest

Your heart begins to race

As you gently moan for more

You are mesmerized by my passion


As I caress your body

I remove your jeans


As the sensation intensifies

I slowly climb on top

Penetrating your body


I massage my chest

Staring into your eyes

The temperature rises as we reach ecstasy

I gently unleash myself from your body


Then I blink

Look away

And reality appears

But my fantasy still remains

# Intertwined

---

A pair of souls meet
Sexual attraction ignites
Their eyes softly caress each other


As their hands gently touch
Their bodies become entangled


As they explore their souls
The friction between their skin intensifies


As they begin to perspire
The sweat trickles down their bodies
Like rain streaming down the windowpane
They softly moan and express their desires


As their bodies reach ecstasy
They slowly untangle themselves

But never completely let go

Of their burning passion

For each other

# Your Presence

When you're around
I feel safe

When you smile
It's contagious

When you laugh
It fills me with happiness

When you assist me
I feel appreciative

When you confide in me
I feel close

When you're in my house
It feels right

When you hold me
I feel secure


When you hug me goodbye
I feel like you never truly leave

# Our Hearts are Bonded as One

My heart was healed and whole
Patiently waiting for the right connection


You unexpectedly came along
Casually intrigued by my openness


Your heart's keys began opening my doors
Instantly forming a connection


Bonding our hearts
As one

# Self-Love

# A Woman

What allows a woman to let down her guard to a man?
Affection, love, togetherness
The excitement of someone caring and loving the woman she is.


What keeps that woman coming back to a failed relationship?
Love, attraction, future potential
In hopes that the man would love her enough to keep his word.


Why would she believe that temporary change is permanent?
A connection, a child, familiarity
The idea of a family shared as one.


What sparks a woman's strength to move on?
Her self-worth, happiness, the freedom
Being able to find happiness in herself.

# The Melody of an Angel

As the music speaks to my broken heart
I'm at a loss for words


The sadness is clouding my vision
I pray you remove the smoke from my mind


Empower my thoughts to take the right path
Giving me the direction I'm missing


Your memory and inspiration will always be alive
Continuously changing me


Even without
Your presence to guide me

# Alone

A time for reflection

That leads to

Self-improvement and growth


A time for heartache

That leads to

Endless questioning and sleepless nights


A time for frustration

That leads to

Anger and sadness


A time for emotional overload

That leads to

Denial and desperation for the other

A time for celebration

That leads to

A newfound freedom


A time to mingle

That leads to

An entrance into togetherness

# Shattered Glass

The sledgehammer struck her heart
Fiercely with no warning
It shattered like a glass vase
Into a million pieces


She lay on the floor, lifeless in shock
Trying to recover from the blow
She regained her breath
Slowly starting to pick up the pieces


Some were large and easy to see
While others invisible, cutting her skin
There were still a few slivers of her heart
She could never find


She searched for years
But those pieces of her heart were never the same
Until one day, she looked in the mirror

Her lost pieces were the most important
But the hardest to see


Her reflection reminded her that
Self-worth, forgiveness, and love
Were the shattered pieces she had to heal
On her own from within

# Restoring a Heart

The damage to a heart goes deep
Creating walls of emotionlessness


From
Repetitive dishonesty
Endless betrayal
Painful scars


This damage forms a foundation
Bound to fail

The happiness of a heart can mend wounds

Creating walls of strength


From

Regained trust

Loyal commitment

Fulfilling acceptance


A foundation

Bound to succeed

# Music

A spiritual getaway
A cleansing of the soul
An escape from reality


An unconditional friend
A counselor of advice
A shoulder to cry on
An understanding connection


A vibration of movement
A rush of eternal happiness
A wound to the heart
A reality check
A life-changing experience

# Achievement

Goals are set to achieve

They challenge our minds

Change our perspectives

And test our priorities


Goals are accomplished by sacrifice

They require devotion

Encourage responsibility

And strengthen our commitment to success

# Changes

We all begin life with a clean slate
A fresh whole heart that is pure


As we grow, the heart matures
Experiencing emotions
A first crush, a heartbreak, or the betrayal of a friend


When we fall short
Our hearts get destroyed
Like a town after a tornado mangling everything in sight


When this destruction occurs
People can be eternally scarred
An attitude, a different personality, or perspectives may form


This destruction can be
Temporary or permanent
Like a physical scar, your voice, or a smile

But everyone can heal their heart

Whether it's through

A song, self-healing, or a quiet evening gazing at the sunset


Some scars

May never completely heal

But a heart is strong, forgiving,

And strives for the freedom of happiness

# Growing Pains

Learning from our failures
Forces us to make a change


Choosing to be uncomfortable
In effort to do something better


Encouraging ourselves to move forward
In an environment where we can grow

# About the Author

I was born in 1979 in Tacoma, Washington and raised by my parents along with my older sister. After high school, I attended the University of Washington in Seattle. In my senior year, I became pregnant with my son. He was four months old when I graduated with a Bachelor of Arts Degree in Sociology and Speech Communications in 2001.

After graduation, I was a single mother for many years until I married in 2007. A year later, my daughter was born in 2008. I was laid off in the spring of 2009, got divorced in 2010, and struggled on unemployment for a year and a half.

In 2011, I became the Activities Coordinator for the Warrior Transition Battalion on Joint Base Lewis-McChord, helping soldiers rehabilitate. I pursued my interests in project management, receiving my Certified Associate in Project Management in 2014, which helped me become a Program Coordinator, where I helped develop an Education and Training Program. During this time, I remarried in 2016, divorcing again in 2018.

This journey of single parenthood, marriage and divorce has been a struggle. Writing poetry was my way of coping with the trauma, drama, devastations, and successes that came and continues to come from it. I wanted to share my experiences with other single mothers to let them know they are not alone. Children are a blessing and shape us into amazing people. Self-love is most important, so always take a moment to recharge. Even if that means you only have two minutes to go to the bathroom with the door closed. Or taking a time out in your car to cry alone.

Many tragic things happen in life, but find a way to forgive others' shortcomings for your own personal freedom. Learn to accept people and situations and how to forgive others for the pain, anger and stress because it only hurts you. I found peace through self-reflection, laughter, and acceptance that helped me maintain the love in my family, and so can you.

# Thank You

Thank you for spending your time in my thoughts.
I would love to hear from you.

Connect with me on social media.
Instagram@Thoughtsoflisarenee

LinkedIn, Facebook, and TikTok at:
Author Lisa Renee Hutchins

YouTube at:
Thoughts of Lisa Renee Hutchins – Author

Email me your thoughts at Gmail.
thoughtsoflisarenee@gmail.com

www.authorlisareneehutchins.com

Stay amazing, and don't let your past define you!
It is only a lesson learned on your journey to greatness!